SELECTED READINGS FROM

SØREN
KIERKEGAARD

EDITED WITH INTRODUCTION BY
ROBERT VAN DE WEYER

Fleming H. Revell Company
Tarrytown, New York

Fleming H. Revell Company Publishers,
Tarrytown, New York
Copyright © 1991 Hunt & Thorpe
Text © 1991 by Robert van de Weyer
Originally published in the UK by Hunt and Thorpe 1991
First published in North America by Fleming Revell
ISBN 0-8007-7131-1

Illustrations by
Fred Apps, James Barton, Elvira Dadd and Vic Mitchell

Manufactured in the United Kingdom.

1 2 3 4 5 6 7 – 96 95 94 93 92 91

CONTENTS

INTRODUCTION

*S*øren Kierkegaard was a tormented, solitary soul with no friends beyond the beer-swilling companions with whom he used to pass the nights away in the bars of Copenhagen. Yet his writings, often published under a pseudonym, have done more to shape modern Christian attitudes than that of any other single thinker. Indeed many of his ideas and insights, which were fresh and even shocking in his day, are now taken for granted as self-evident truth. Moreover he is justly regarded as the founder of the philosophical movement known as existentialism – although most subsequent existentialists, such as Jean-Paul Sartre, were vigorous atheists.

His life was outwardly uneventful. He was born in Denmark in 1813, the youngest son of an elderly father who had come to Copenhagen as a poor peasant, and earned a large fortune as a merchant. But despite his wealth the father was morbid and gloomy, obsessed with his own sins and terrified of God's judgment. He instilled in his own children the same terror, a burden from which Søren never entirely escaped. However, once at university, Søren soon rebelled against his father's morality, drinking heavily and frequenting the sleazier brothels of the city. He also began going to the theater and reading the great literature of Europe, so that by his early twenties he could present himself as a cultured man of the world.

In 1838, at the age of twenty-five, he entered a

prolonged period of spiritual crisis. His father confessed to him that the source of his fear of God's wrath was that as a young man he had made a curse against God, compelling him to share his father's guilt. Shortly afterwards his father died, And in his confusion of guilt and grief he became engaged to a young woman called Regina Olsen. But, far from bringing peace, his anguish deepened, as if he felt himself unworthy of her; and in l841 he broke off the engagement.

Throughout this period he kept a journal which is a mixture of biting aphorisms about religious hypocrisy and profound reflections on his own condition. But by the early 1840s his spirit was sufficiently settled for him to embark on the most creative period of his career. In l843 he published *Either/Or* in which he presented life as a chain between blind enjoyment of earth's pleasure, and self-realization through inner contemplation. He rejected any kind of middle way, asserting that each of us must fall on one or the other side. This was a theme which persisted in all his writings, gradually coming to be presented as a stark decision for or against Christ.

Two other major themes permeate his writings. Firstly his assertion of Christ as a contemporary, rather than a historical, figure. For him the fact that God became man is the matter of vital importance, transcending historical questions of time and place; and it is to this fact that we are called to respond. Secondly he was angrily opposed to the notion of "Christendom" where Christianity is the established religion in which the radical choice which Jesus presents is lost beneath pious and comforting platitudes. Indeed he had little time for any kind of institutional religion, regarding all forms of religious organization as a means of hiding the true nature of human life.

He died in 1855 aged forty-two, mourned by no one. For many years few read his writings, and his name was almost forgotten. But in the early years of this century he was discovered by philosophers and theologians, hailed by both as a prophet, a century ahead of his time. Like so many profound thinkers, his books and essays are often tortuous and obscure. yet the essential ideas are bright and clear, and in this collection I have attempted to extract those passages in which he expresses himself most succinctly. In his own life he could be accused of hypocrisy, manifestly flouting the moral demands of Christ. Yet he judged himself more harshly than he ever judged others, and in struggling with his own burden of guilt he wrestled, like Jacob, with God himself.

Thereafter books and essays poured unceasingly from his pen. He liked to keep up appearances as a dissolute aesthete, spending his evenings drinking or at the theater, and he continued to make use of prostitutes. Yet as the years passed, Christianity took over from philosophy as the focus of his concern. He had no desire for fame, and saw himself in conversation with the individual reader. And such an attitude to authorship accorded with his existentialism, which regarded each individual as entirely free, morally and spiritually able to determine the course of their lives. Kierkegaard saw himself not as advocating Christianity, but as presenting clearly and honestly the moral and spiritual choice which Jesus presents to the individual.

Yet the choice is far from straightforward; it is filled with paradox. The most basic paradox is of life and death: on the face of it Jesus offers us suffering and death, yet this is the only route to true and lasting joy. Connected to this is the paradox of humility and glory: Jesus speaks to us as a man of humility, sharing our despair and confusion; we respond to him in his glory, as God who offers us new birth. There is the paradox of love and self-love: while selfishness is the opposite of love, self-love is the essential foundation of love, since only insofar as we love ourselves can we truly love others. There is the paradox of emotion and duty: it is emotion which first stimulates us to love; and yet love can only be sustained as a matter of duty, an act of will, which can seem to be the antithesis of love. And, most striking of all is the way in which Kierkegaard handles the paradox of reason and faith: reason may take us to the edge of faith, but ultimately religion defies human logic; only by a "leap of faith" can we commit ourselves to Christ.

1
Personal reflections

Kierkegaard never intended that his Journals should
be published. Yet they contain some of his most
moving writings, as well as some of his sharpest wit.
Even when he was apparently writing objectively, the
real subject is himself. So when he reflects on sin, he
is grappling with his own guilt. When he writes about
the dangers to a child of having a pious father, he is
remembering his own upbringing. And when he
discusses man's sensuous nature, he is expressing
his own ambivalence about earthly pleasures.

THE HOPE OF YOUTH

*T*he whole of existence frightens me, from the smallest fly to the mystery of the Incarnation. Everything is unintelligible to me, most of all myself. The whole of existence seems corrupt, especially myself. My sorrow knows no bounds; no man can understand it, only God in heaven, and he will not console me. No man can console me, only God in heaven, and he will not take pity on me. I am a young man, at the beginning of the path of life. Let me turn to him, that he may prepare me for manhood. Let me not waste my youth in rebellion against him. Let me not exhaust my young spirit by seeking solace in evil things. Let my sad soul be pierced by the arrows of his love.

WATERS OF PEACE

*M*ost people first try to find themselves outside themselves. They seek fulfilment through work, wealth and status. Then eventually that route takes them to the rock of despair, in which their souls are broken. Only as their souls break do they turn upwards to God, and then can see the way to the calm waters of his peace.

WATERS OF LIFE

*I*f an Arab in the desert were suddenly to discover a spring in his tent, and so would always be able to have water in abundance, how fortunate he would consider himself. So too when a man turns inwards, and looks for the waters of life within his own soul, he has been truly blessed by God.

SIN AND HUMAN NATURE

*S*ometimes people are led astray as to what sin is, often by a most well-meaning person. For example, a father may explain to his son that sexual desire is sinful. This may have become true for his father because in his case sexual desire leads to promiscuity and violence. But sexual desire in itself is neither good nor sinful; it is part of human nature. Sin is an act of will, not an aspect of nature.

CHRISTIAN UPBRINGING

*T*he greatest danger for a child, where religion is concerned, is not that his father should be an atheist or even a hypocrite. No, the danger lies in his being a pious, Godfearing man, and yet who nonetheless has deep in his soul an unrest and discontent which neither piety nor the fear of God can calm. The child will observe this, and conclude that God is not infinite love.

BAPTISM OF FORGETFULNESS

*M*y grief is like a castle, which is built high up on a mountain peak among the clouds: nothing can storm it. My grief is like an eagle's nest, on the highest branches: from it I fly down to seize my prey, which is the misery of life itself, and I carry that misery back into the nest. But I long to immerse my grief in the baptism of forgetfulness, in which everything finite is erased, and that which is eternal will rise up within my soul.

THE SOURCE OF DESPAIR

A despairing man despairingly wants to be himself, he will not want to get rid of himself – or so it seems. But if one inspects more closely, one perceives a contradiction. The self which he despairingly wishes to be is a self which he is not – for to wish to be the self that one truly is is the opposite of despair. The despairing man wants to tear himself away from the Power that created him. But he can never do this because the Power is too strong, and compels him to be the self that he truly is. If only he could see this truth, he would be freed from despair, and joyfully accept his own true self.

OUR SENSUOUS NATURE

*I*t is far from being the case that men in general regard finding the truth as the highest good. Their sensuous nature usually dominates their spiritual nature. So when a man is enjoying sensuous pleasure he imagines himself to be happy: and in most cases that illusion is very strong. Indeed any attempt to shatter that illusion provokes fury, and those who try to shatter that illusion are regarded as enemies, as kill-joys. This is because the sensuous person has no other categories in which to understand experience than pleasure and pain. So he hates the person that denies him pleasure.

FORGETTING OUR SINS

*I*t requires more courage to suffer than to act. It takes more courage to forget than to remember. The most wonderful quality of God is that he can forget men's sins.

CHEATING ABOUT LIFE

*T*here are many people who reach their conclusions about life like schoolboys. They cheat their teacher by copying the answer out of a book, without having worked it out for themselves.

CASTLES IN THE AIR

*I*n relation to their philosophical systems, most philosophers are like a man who builds an enormous castle, and lives in a shack close by. They do not live by their enormous philosophical systems. Christianity offers only a draughty stable in which to live; and the true Christian joyfully lives within it.

SIMPLE PLEASURE

The essence of pleasure does not lie in the thing enjoyed, but in our attitude to it. The person who rejoices in simplicity will find no pleasure in riches. If the simple person asks for a glass of water, and receives the finest wine in the costliest chalice, it will not give pleasure, but pain. We shall enjoy the greatest pleasure in this life if we learn to love the simplest things.

2
The leap of faith

As a philosopher Kierkegaard would like to have been able to prove the truth of Christianity. But his honesty compelled him to recognize that, far from being rational, becoming a Christian requires a "leap of faith," taking one beyond the realm of logic. This leap can only be made by the individual, responding to the spirit within him. Thus Kierkegaard insisted that Christianity is "subjective". The following extracts are from "Philosophical Fragments" and "Postscript," published in 1844 and 1846 respectively.

OBJECTIVE UNCERTAINTY

Without risk there is no faith. Faith is the contradiction between the infinite passion of the person's inward spirit and objective uncertainty. If I were capable of grasping God objectively, I would not believe. But since I cannot grasp him objectively, I must believe. If I wish to preserve myself in faith, I must constantly be intent upon holding fast objective uncertainty, so in the objective uncertainty I am swimming in deep water – and yet believe.

THE PASSIONATE CHOICE

*I*n Christianity there is both choice and no choice, freedom and compulsion. Christianity says to a man, "you shall choose to accept the essential truth of life"; and this truth is so compelling that you have no choice. Indeed once you perceive this essential truth, you have no choice but to accept it. Once you realize that God is inviting you into his kingdom, you cannot refuse. The choice to accept or reject Christianity is not a matter of cool deliberation, weighing up pros and cons with the intellect. Christ demands a response of infinite passion, either of hatred or of love. Those who crucified him responded with hatred. If you respond with love, you cannot help but accept his invitation. Thus the choice is of passion, not of reason.

GOD LOVES THE LEARNER

*T*hose who seek to love the truth are the true objects of God's love. God desires to teach them, and to bring them into equality with himself. If this equality cannot be achieved, God's love becomes unhappy and his teaching futile, because his happiness consists in mutual understanding betweer himself and those who learn. Men sometimes imagine that their condition is a matter of indifference to God, since he does not stand in need of the learner. But in this we are ignorant – or, rather, we show how far we are from understanding him. We forget that God loves the learner, and so grieves when the learner cannot grasp the truth. God grieves that the learner may be so caught up in guilt and corruption that he finds him repulsive. God desires that the learner should sustain his courage and trust, in the hope that every barrier to mutual understanding shall be broken down.

SUBJECTIVE TRUTH

*C*hristianity proposes to endow the individual with an eternal happiness, a good which is not distributed wholesale, but only to one individual at a time. Christianity answers that in each individual there is a potential to appreciate and receive this gift. But it does not answer that the individual is immediately ready to receive it, because many people do not understand its significance. A person must first realize that God communicates with him as an individual. Thus Christianity is subjective, protesting against every form of objectivity. It desires that the individual be infinitely concerned with himself, because it is within the self that truth is to be found. Christianity is not a system of doctrines which can be objectively proven to be correct. Christianity is the receipt by one individual at a time of the gift of eternal joy, through the discovering within the self of eternal truth.

SEEKING GOD

*L*et us compare two people seeking God. The first seeks God objectively, pursuing the idea of God through reason and logic. The second is driven by the infinite passion of his need for God, and feels an infinite concern for his own relationship with God. It is not possible to be both objective and subjective. The first goes to the house of God to pray, but prays in a false spirit. The second may even be worshipping an idol, but prays in a true spirit.

PASSIONATE RESPONSE

*C*hristianity has declared itself to be the eternal, essential truth which has come into being in time. It requires an inwardness of faith which is an offense to the Jews and folly to the Greeks. It requires courage to believe that which is logically absurd. Yet it would surely be very strange if Christianity had come into the world just to offer a logical explanation of things, as if Jesus himself were merely a philosopher. Christianity came into the world to demand a passionate response from each individual.

THE INFINITY OF GOD

What is true of the relationship between two people is not true of the relationship of an individual to God. In the case of two people, the longer they live together, the better they know each other, and the closer they come to one another. But the very opposite is true in relation to God. The longer one lives with him, the more infinite he becomes – and the smaller one becomes by comparison. To a child it seems as if God and man can play together. To a youth it seems as if emotional passion for God could bring perfect union with him. But to an adult God is Infinitely vast, and the distance between man and God infinitely great.

THE CONFINEMENT OF FAITH

When faith in God begins to affect an individual, his entire existence is transformed. His obsession with immediate pleasures and pains dies away. Instead his attention is increasingly focused on God. He comes to conceive God in his heart not just at a particular moment, but at every moment. He desires to share the infinity of God, and so feels himself confined within his present existence. He is like a bird in a cage, dreaming of flying free; he is like a fish on dry land, dreaming of swimming and well. He is acutely aware of the contrast between God's power and his own frailty. Yet even in his confinement, he feels joy in the knowledge that soon he will be free.

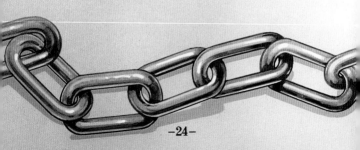

THE CHRISTIAN AND THE LOVER

The acceptance of Christian doctrine does not make a person Christian. Becoming a Christian depends on living with Christ and dying with him. Indeed the true Christian has no interest in doctrine, which is little more than an attempt to define that which is beyond definition. Just as a lover would never try to define his love, so a believer will never try to define his faith. Indeed, there is no difference between a lover and a Christian: both are filled with inward passion.

ERUDITION AND FAITH

The Christian who becomes too concerned with theology is liable to confuse erudition with faith, knowledge with truth. He is liable to think that words can capture God, and logic can define existence. He will never realize that inward passion which is the mark of faith. In the case of a lover, it is a sure sign that passion is waning when the lover wishes to treat the object of his love objectively. Passion and reflection generally exclude each other. Becoming objective is our way of avoiding truth, because the truth threatens our comfort. The passion for truth is man's perdition; but it is his exaltation also.

3

Works of love

Although he often described himself as a poet, Kierkegaard spurned what he regarded as a "poetic" view of love. The majority of people, he asserted, follow the poets in seeing love as an emotion. But to Kierkegaard emotional love is inevitably transient leading to hatred and despair. Only when love is a "duty," by which he meant an act of will, does it reflect the eternal love of God. Yet he objected also to those Christians who interpret that duty as implying that one should love one's neighbor more than oneself. To Kierkegaard love of one's neighbor must be rooted in self-love. These reflections on love are taken from *Works of Love*, published in 1847.

LOVING OTHERS AS YOURSELF

*C*hrist commands you to "love your neighbor as yourself." But this "as yourself"? Certainly no wrestler can get so tight a clinch upon his opponent as that which this commandment gets on our selfish hearts. The commandment is so easy to understand, and yet we must be broken in spirit to follow it. As Jacob limped after he had wrestled with God, so shall our selfishness be broken when it has wrestled with this commandment. Yet this commandment does not teach that a man should not love himself. Rather, it teaches him the proper kind of self-love. Christianity presupposes that a man loves himself, and adds that in loving himself he should also love his neighbor.

SELF-LOVE

Would it not be possible to love one's neighbor better than oneself? We hear people saying that this is possible when they are filled with enthusiasm. Could it be that Christianity fails to soar so high because it addresses itself to simple ordinary people? Is Christianity a feeble faith that it does not demand such a high standard of love? Certainly no poet has ever sung about loving one's neighbor, nor sung about loving him as oneself. Perhaps we should be grateful that Christianity sets a low standard that is easy to reach. Certainly not! In truth it is impossible to love one's neighbor more than oneself, because love of others can grow only out of proper self-love. You cannot love your neighbor and hate yourself.

LOVING GOD

There is only one being whom a man may love better than himself: God. Therefore Christ does not say "Love God as yourself," but "Love God with all your heart, soul and mind." A man must give God unconditional obedience, and adore him with unstinting love. It would be idolatry if a man dared to love himself in this way, and, worse still, dared to persuade another person to love him in this way. If a friend asked you for something which you knew would harm him, then love would not demand unconditional obedience, but rather disobedience. But when God demands something which seems to be harmful, then we must obey him, trusting in his mercy. God's wisdom is infinitely greater than our wisdom, so his providence is not answerable to our calculations.

THE NEIGHBOR

Who then is one's neighbor? The neighbor is the one who is nearer to you than all others. But is he also nearer to you than you are to yourself? No; but he is, or should be, equally near. The concept "neighbor" is really an extension of your own self. Indeed it is not even necessary that the neighbor should actually exist. If a man lived on a desert island, and developed his mind and heart in harmony with this commandment, then he could still be said to love his neighbor. He would achieve this by truly loving himself.

TAKING LOVE FOR GRANTED

Christ says, "You shall love." This commandment has been in force for eighteen hundred years since Christ first spoke it. Now everyone is brought up to it, yet our attitude to the commandment is like that of a child brought up in a rich home who easily forgets that his daily bread is a gift. Christianity, and the teachings of Christ, are taken for granted, so that we easily forget that they are the source of life and happiness. To use another comparison, we are like people who prefer sweets to wholesome food. We prefer the quick and easy pleasure of life, to the profound joy of faith.

THE DUTY OF LOVE

*O*nly when love is a duty is it eternally secure. The sense of duty drives out all doubt and anxiety, because it excludes all possibility of change; whereas love based on emotion and feeling can change, and so is not secure. Emotional love may for a period be so intense that the heart burns with passion; but in that passion there is always anxiety that eventually the fire will burn itself out. This anxiety leads us constantly to test the other's love, to reassure oneself that all is well. But this testing is a sign of lack of confidence. Yet if love is a duty, a binding commitment before God, then there is no need to test. Emotions and feelings may come and go; but dutiful love lasts forever.

HATE

*E*motional love can easily be changed into its opposite, hate. Hate is not lack of love; rather it is love turned into its opposite. The heart continues to burn with emotion – but with the emotion of hate, not of love. Yet such a love cannot be true love, because true love is eternal and unchanging. True love is simple: it makes no calculations, it does not count the cost, it does not doubt. It may seem at times that emotional love is stronger, because it is more intense. But we should not confuse intensity with strength. Intense love can turn into intense hate. Strong love remains always strong.

JEALOUSY

*E*motional love often breeds jealousy, and so causes agony. Emotional love seeks to possess the beloved, and so ultimately seeks to destroy the beloved. Thus if the beloved refuses to be a possession, the heart is on fire with jealousy. The jealous person does not hate the beloved, but is tortured with the fear of the beloved breaking free. The jealous person pleads for reassurance from the beloved, rejoicing in every sign of warmth. But this warmth only adds to the fire of jealousy by increasing the desire to possess the beloved, yet paradoxically, if the beloved is willing to be possessed, this does not quench the agony. Rather the jealousy turns to contempt, since a person who is possessed by another loses all individuality, all the qualities that may evoke love.

THE FORCE OF HABIT

*E*motional love changes over the years. It loses its ardor, its intensity, its desire, its freshness. The path of emotional love is like a river. It starts as a spring, pure and clear, bubbling out of a rock; but eventually it spreads out, becomes slow and muddy. Of all the enemies of love, force of habit is the most crafty, because it is so easy to ignore; indeed once we see a habit we are saved from it. Habit is not like other enemies which one can struggle against. It creeps up stealthily on its victim, and, like a vampire bite, sucks the blood out of love without being noticed. Habits make us comfortable; but they also destroy our love.

THE POWER OF FORGIVENESS

*W*hy is forgiveness so rare? Is it because people do not believe in the power of forgiveness? Even a man who is not inclined to bear malice or spite is often heard to say: "I could readily forgive him, but I do not see how that would help." Yet if you have ever truly felt the need of forgiveness yourself, then you know what forgiveness can do. To forgive another person does not consist in regarding yourself as morally superior to that person; and to seek forgiveness does not imply moral inferiority. Every person bears a burden of guilt, and that burden can only be lifted by forgiveness. When forgiveness takes place a miracle of faith occurs. Faith can move mountains; faith, expressed in forgiveness, can move the mountain of guilt.

FORGIVING AND FORGETTING

When God forgives, he forgets. To forget something does not imply ignorance of it, because one cannot forget what one has never known. That which is forgotten was known. Forgetting is in this sense not the opposite of remembering, but of fearing. When a sin is remembered, we fear the consequence; when a sin is forgotten, that fear disappears. Thus through forgetting, fear turns to hope – hope in God's mercy and love. When God forgets our sins he puts the process of creation into reverse: we have created the sin; he turns the sin back into nothing. In the same way we must forgive one another, by forgetting each other's sins, blotting them out, erasing them.

THE QUALITY OF LOVE

To have love is to presuppose love in others; to be loving is to presuppose that others are loving. A man may have many gifts and talents which do not presuppose that they are present in others. A man may be wise, but this does not mean that those around him are wise: wisdom is a quality inherent in itself. But if a man were to imagine himself loving, yet find that all others were not loving, there would be a contradiction. Love cannot be isolated, it cannot exist in only one person's heart. Love is the mutual response that binds people. It is the quality that lifts humanity from being a mere collection of individuals to being a society, a culture, a civilization. And Christianity exists to embody and proclaim that truth.

4
Training in Christianity

Kierkegaard believed his greatest work was *Training in Christianity*, published in 1850, and certainly it was his most radical. It rejects all claims that Christianity rests on the historical accuracy of the gospels. Instead, Kierkegaard believed the Christian must respond to the "contemporary" Christ, present in spirit here and now. The essence of Christianity is that God became man; and this truth transcends history and culture, and defies any historical account. In his own day Kierkegaard's view was little less than blasphemy. But by the early twentieth century many scholars had accepted that the quest for the historical Christ is ultimately fruitless – and that Kierkegaard's theology offers a far more solid foundation for faith.

THE CONTEMPORARY CHRIST

*I*t is eighteen hundred years or more since Jesus Christ walked on earth. But this was not an event like other events which, once past, disappears into the mist of history. No. His presence here on earth never becomes mere history, and never recedes into the mist of time. Or rather, to a person without faith Jesus is indeed only an historical figure. But to a person with faith Jesus is contemporary: he lives here and now, just as he lived here and now for the first disciples. This contemporaneousness is a condition of faith. Or, more precisely, it is faith.

MOVEMENTS OF FAITH

I can, I think, describe the movements of faith perfectly, but that does not mean I can perform them. A person could describe the movements of swimming perfectly, but that does not mean he can swim. Christianity reveals the movements of infinity; faith consists of imitating those movements in this finite world. Blessed is he who can make these movements of faith, because thereby he performs a miracle.

UNCERTAINTY AND FAITH

*I*f a person could be certain that God would use him as his instrument, as a king uses a minister, then he would submit willingly to every sacrifice. But it is not possible to have real certainty in one's relationship with God. One can only have a spiritual relationship with a Spirit, and that by its nature is intangible, and hence uncertain. Faith is the bridge between uncertainty and truth.

CHRIST THE HELPER

When a person needs help of any kind, he seeks out someone who has the ability to help him. He might beg that person to help him out of the goodness of his heart; but more usually he must pay for the help he receives. The helper thus sets a high value on himself. Jesus Christ by contrast never needs to be sought. He knows our needs before we know them ourselves, and he is offering to help us before we ask. He sets no value on himself, but gives himself totally to us without asking any reward. And we soon discover that he is the only one who can help us in our deepest needs.

THE COMPASSION OF CHRIST

To help the poor, one must have known poverty, and so understand their condition. To help the naked and homeless, one must have experienced the desolation of being cold, with nowhere to rest one's head. To help the sick, one must have suffered even to the point of death. To help the oppressed, one must have been arrested unjustly, and sentenced to death for crimes one did not commit. Jesus Christ has experienced all these things. He has been poor, and homeless, he has suffered the most terrible agonies, and he has died an innocent victim. He is our perfect helper, because he can sympathize with all our needs.

CHRIST'S ANXIETY

*C*hrist's deepest concern is that there are some who will never hear his invitation. He has no fear that too many will come, because he can receive all who seek his help. But he is anxious that some will be blinded by prejudice against him. He is anxious that some will be too proud to seek his help, imagining they are strong enough on their own. He is worried that those who convey his invitation will fail to convince people that the help is offered free. Above all, he is anxious that people will be so absorbed by the pleasures of this world that they will scoff at his invitation.

THE CROSSROADS

*C*hrist's invitation is like a sign at a crossroads. In one direction the road may seem smooth and easy, but in fact is soft and boggy; so despite appearances the path is hard, and eventually one sinks wholly into the mud. In the other direction it seems rough and hard, scattered with boulders and sharp stones, and in the distance one can see rushing rivers to cross. Christ invites us into the rough road, promising to cast aside the stones and carry us over the rivers. The question is whether we trust his promise.

TWO LIVES

*T*he invitation of Christ comes at the parting of the ways, where one life divides from another life. As a child life is one: at the mother's breast sensuous pleasure is perfectly mingled with spiritual love. But as an adult a life dedicated to the pursuit of pleasure can no longer be mingled with the life of Christ's love. Christ does not deny us pleasure; on the contrary, life in Christ is filled with pleasure. But in Christ pleasure is never sought, only received. Christ himself, and the truth which he embodies, becomes the sole object of our desire; and if he chooses to encourage us with moments of earthly joy, then we can only offer our thanks.

THE JUDGMENT OF HISTORY

*I*f a man is persecuted by the people of his age, it does not follow that he has a right to say that this would have happened to him in any age. Indeed posterity may say, "Let us now forget that this man died unjustly." Very different, however, is the case of Jesus Christ! The reason is that he does not submit himself to this judgment. He is the judge of history, and his life is the judgment. And he judges not just his own race and generation, but every race and every generation. We should never forget that he died unjustly, for that injustice is the judgment on our sins.

PAST AND PRESENT

*J*esus Christ insists on being a definite historical person, who lived eighteen hundred years ago in a world quite different from our own. But we do not learn about him merely from history. In truth history teaches us absolutely nothing about Christ, for Christ cannot be understood in terms of historical fact. He refuses to be judged by the standards of history, which would dismiss him as an insignificant preacher in an insignificant land. He refuses to be judged by the consequences of his earthly life, which were the merest ripple on the surface of history. He can only be understood as above and beyond history, as infinitely present at every moment.

FAITH AND REASON

*I*s it possible to conceive of a more foolish enterprise than to try and prove that a definite historical individual was God? It is an offense to human reason for an individual to declare himself God and to be God. To try to prove such a thing would be to turn logic on its head. One can only prove that an individual was, and is, God by defying reason. The proofs which Scripture presents for Christ's divinity – his miracles, his resurrection from the dead, his ascension into heaven – are proofs only for the eyes of faith. They prove only that Christ's divinity is a matter of faith.

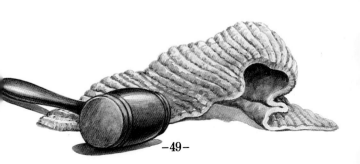

THE SUFFERING SERVANT

When God came as Jesus Christ, in the form of a servant, this was no mere outer garb. God chose to suffer all things, endure all things, experience all things. He chose to suffer hunger in the desert, to thirst during his time of agony, to be forsaken in death, to be humiliated. Death itself was not the source of his suffering; throughout his life on earth he suffered. It was through love that he suffered, the love which gives everything, What wonderful self-denial! Any other form of revelation would be a deception, because it would not show the true nature of God.

THE IMPORTANCE OF CHRIST

There is nothing noteworthy in the fact that a man lived; millions upon millions of people have lived. If this fact is to become noteworthy, the man's life must acquire some noteworthy distinction, his life must have important consequences. But the fact that God lived here on earth as an individual man is infinitely noteworthy. Even if it had no consequences whatever, even if only a few people were aware of him it would still be infinitely noteworthy. The fact that God lived on earth is in itself of infinite importance. Assume that Christ's life had no historical consequences, that no important historical facts remained about him. Christ would still be the most important figure in the history of the world.

THE MISFORTUNE OF CHRISTENDOM

*T*he misfortune of Christendom is that it has encouraged people in the notion that by knowing the facts about Christ's life eighteen hundred years ago, they have faith. By degrees, as knowledge about Christ became accepted as faith, so all the pith and vigor went out of Christianity; the tension of the paradox of faith was slackened; one became a Christian without noticing it; the offense of Christianity was ignored. One took possession of Christian doctrine, turned it about and inspected it, while the meaning of Jesus Christ himself was lost. Becoming a Christian became as simple as thrusting a foot into a stocking. And in this way Christianity became paganism. On Sunday clergymen in the pulpit talk a lot of twaddle about Christianity's glorious and priceless truths, and the sweet consolation which it offers. But it is only too evident that the Jesus Christ to whom they refer is merely an historical figure, not a living reality.

THE MADDNESS OF CHRISTIANITY

What is the use of Christianity? Is it a mere plague to us? Yes, in a sense it is the worst plague that could ever afflict us. In moments of laxness, laziness, dullness, when our sensuous nature predominates, Christianity seems madness – absolute madness, yet this precisely is its value. Christianity is the absolute, and so it must be preached as if it were madness. When the clever man dismisses Christ by saying "he is nothing," he is correct: by all relative standards, Christ is indeed nothing. He cannot be compared with all the "somethings" that make up the world. Christianity came into the world not as an historical accident, not as a consolation to troubled souls – although it is rooted in history, and does offer consolation. It stands above history, above transient human feelings. It is the absolute.

TRANSFORMED IN CHRIST

There is an endless yawning gap between God and man. Hence to become a Christian, to be transformed into the likeness of God, is to endure greater torment and misery than the greatest human misery. It thus seems a crime in the view of one's neighbors. And so it will always be, so long as becoming a Christian means living alongside the living Christ. Indeed if Christianity does not mean this, it is nonsense, self-deception and deceit. In relation to Christ, the absolute, there cannot be past and future, only the present. And it is in responding to the ever-present Christ that we find our whole nature pulled about, battered, molded, shaped in the form of Christ.

5
Attack on Christendom

In Kierkegaard's time the idea of the "Christian nation," whose religion was upheld by the State, was still broadly accepted. Respectable people had their children baptized and supported the church, believing that it upheld the nation's morals. Kierkegaard angrily rejected such a religion, regarding it as a mockery of the Christianity of the New Testament. Since Christianity is the subjective response of the individual to Christ, there can be no such thing as a Christian nation. On the contrary Christianity must be an "offense" to all forms of official religion, demanding a total transformation of values and attitudes. His *Attack upon Christendom* was his last major work, published in 1855.

THE RESPECTABLE CHRISTIAN

*L*et us imagine a young man who is a skilled businessman, cultured and well-spoken, with an interest in public affairs. As for religion, he feels no need. It never occurs to him to think of God, nor does he go to church. He does not object to religion, but he fears that to read the Bible would make him appear ridiculous. But then he decides to get married and soon is a father. He wants his children to be baptized, and to grow up with correct moral standards. And he feels that it is the church's job to teach those standards. So he sends his children for religious education. Soon he is regarded as a pillar of the church, supporting its work generously and playing a leading role in its management. He is universally regarded as a good Christian. But still he feels no need of religion, nor does he ever think of God.

SUNDAY AND MONDAY

In church on Sunday the clergyman will say: "You must not depend on the world, nor upon me, nor upon yourself, but you must depend wholly on God; for a human being by himself can do nothing." And we all understand it, for it is easy to understand. Indeed it is frightening how easily we can understand it in principle, when we hear it on Sunday, But on Monday it becomes very difficult, because then we must try to apply it to daily life. Then it is easy to ignore it, allowing our humble intentions to fade away, and be replaced by pride in our own strength.

ILLUSORY CHRISTIANITY

We are what is called a Christian nation. But this Christianity is not that of the New Testament. The illusion of a Christian nation is due to the power which numbers exact. I am quite sure that most people in the nation are honest enough to say, to themselves at least: "I do not deny that, I am not a Christian in the New Testament sense. I do not renounce the world. I am not willing to die for Christ. On the contrary earthly pleasure is more important to me than spiritual truth." Yet these same people will equally assert that they try to lead good lives, earning the respect of the neighbors, and like to have the label Christian applied to them. When millions upon millions are like this, we describe the nation as Christian, and we talk of ourselves living in Christendom. It is a most dangerous confusion.

OUTWARD RELIGION

The established Church tries to satisfy people's spiritual wants before they feel them. It offers spiritual care to people's souls before they desire such care. It has all the outward aspects of true religion, yet its adherents do not want the inward essence, That is why the religion offered by the established Church is an empty shell. It may be compared with a man who eats a huge amount of food, and yet gets thinner and thinner. The established Church conducts a huge amount of religion, yet the inner spirit wastes away. And the parsons of the established Church delude themselves that this is the faith which Jesus Christ taught.

THE GOD-MAN

*I*n the early ages of Christianity the various heresies about the person of Christ showed unmistakably that even the heretics had a firm grasp of the essence of Christianity. Some overemphasized his divine nature, making him too remote from human experience, Others over-emphasized his human nature, making God too remote. But all focused on Christ himself. Today the person of Jesus Christ is almost lost to view. The enthusiastic Christians concentrate on the Bible, referring to it as the Word of God, forgetting that it is Christ who is the Word. The majority simply reduce Christianity to a series of moral maxims. Christianity is nothing unless we put our faith in Christ as the God-Man.

6

Prayers

Kierkegaard's prayers are dotted throughout his works. They do not lend themselves to use in public worship or even in private devotion. But they offer a deep insight into a soul often in torment, and always striving to apply the faith in practice.

CHRIST'S INFINITE PATIENCE

Through your whole life, O Lord Jesus Christ, you suffered that I might be saved. And yet your suffering is not at an end. For still you have to bear with me, stumbling as I walk along the path, and constantly going astray. How often have I become impatient, wanting to give up your way! And how often have you given me the encouragement and helping hand that I need. Every day I increase the burden that you must bear; but just as I am impatient so you are infinitely patient.

COVERING OUR SINS

Your love covers the multitude of my sins. So when I am fully aware of my sin, when before the justice of heaven only wrath is pronounced upon me, then you are the only person to whom I can escape. If I try to cover myself against the guilt of sin and the wrath of heaven, I will be driven to madness and despair. But if I rely on you to cover my sins, I shall find peace and joy. You suffered and died on the cross to shelter us from our guilt, and take upon yourself the wrath that we deserve. Let me rest under you, and may you transform me into your likeness.

CHRIST THE HIDING-PLACE

The birds have their nests and the foxes their holes. But you were homeless, Lord Jesus, with nowhere to rest your head. And yet you were a hiding-place where the sinner could flee. Today you are still such a hiding-place, and I flee to you. I hide myself under your wings, and your wings cover the multitude of my sins.

FROM YOUR HAND

From your hand, O Lord, we receive everything. You stretch your powerful hand, and turn worldly wisdom into holy folly. You open your gentle hand, and offer the gift of inward peace. If sometimes it seems that your arm is shortened, then you increase our faith and trust, so that we may reach out to you. And if sometimes it seems that you withdraw your hand from us, then we know that it is only to conceal the eternal blessing which you have promised – that we may yearn even more fervently for that blessing.

OUR WEAKNESS, YOUR STRENGTH

*T*here is much to drag us back, O Lord: empty pursuits, trivial pleasures, unworthy cares. There is much to frighten us away: pride that makes us reluctant to accept help; cowardice that recoils from sharing your suffering; anguish at the prospect of confessing our sins to you. But you are stronger than all these forces. We call you our redeemer and savior because you redeem us from our empty, trivial existence, you save us from our foolish fears. This is your work which you have completed and will continue to complete every moment.

SEE YOU AS YOU ARE

O Lord Jesus Christ, I long to live in your presence, to see your human form and to watch you walking on earth. I do not want to see you through the darkened glass of tradition, nor through the eyes of today's values and prejudices. I want to see you as you were, as you are, and as you always will be. I want to see you as an offense to human pride, as a man of humility, walking amongst the lowliest of men, and yet as the savior and redeemer of the human race.